About the Book

Underwater exploration is described and pictured in this fascinating study that begins with man's early attempts to breathe and survive in deep water and concludes with current and proposed experiments for cities under the sea. The author tells about underwater equipment, machinery, and vehicles, and shows how they are used for such purposes as exploration, rescue, retrieval, and farming.

Illustrated by Vincent Colabella

MEN UNDER THE SEA

Anabel Dean

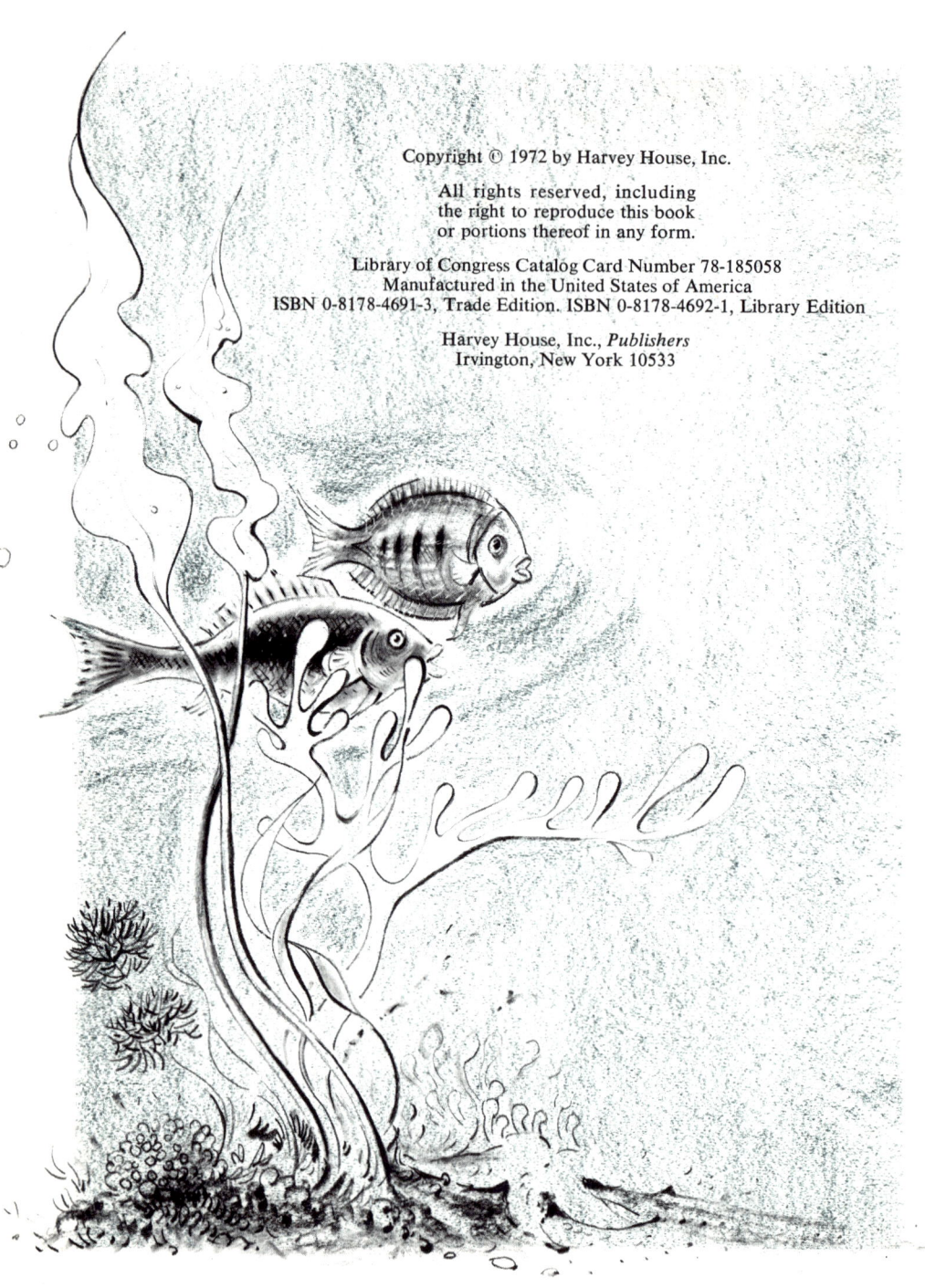

Copyright © 1972 by Harvey House, Inc.

All rights reserved, including
the right to reproduce this book
or portions thereof in any form.

Library of Congress Catalog Card Number 78-185058
Manufactured in the United States of America
ISBN 0-8178-4691-3, Trade Edition. ISBN 0-8178-4692-1, Library Edition

Harvey House, Inc., *Publishers*
Irvington, New York 10533

CONTENTS

The Sea and Man	9
Diving Bells	11
Deep Sea Diving	15
Skin Diving	18
The Submarine	23
The Bathysphere	25
The Bathyscaphe	27
Submersibles	28
Too Many People	32
Conshelf	34
Man-in-the-Sea	38

The Sea and Man

For thousands of years people have lived near oceans and rivers. Food was plentiful there, and they could move in boats from one place to another easier than they could move about on land.

Oceans help keep the earth's climate from becoming too hot or cold. Water absorbs heat from the sun and then gives it off again very slowly. This helps to cool the land in summer and to warm it in winter.

As ocean water evaporates, some of it goes up into the air and forms clouds. The winds blow the wet air over the land and it falls to the ground as rain or snow.

Some of the water remains on the land to be used by plants, animals and man. Most of it makes its way back to the ocean again through rivers and streams. This is called the *water cycle*.

Men have always wanted to see beneath oceans and inland seas. Pearl divers often told about strange things under the water, but they could never stay under long enough for a satisfying look.

Diving Bells

Thousands of years ago someone discovered that by holding a tub upside-down over his head while wading out into the water, he could breathe the air trapped inside the tub. Of course, with a tub over his head, he could only see straight down. For a long time this was the only known method of breathing under water, and was probably the earliest type of diving bell.

The air pressure inside the tub kept the water from coming up into it. Using a cork, a glass, and a large glass jar half-filled with water, you can prove this yourself.

Float the cork in the jar of water. Now turn the glass upside down and press it down over the cork. You will see the level of the water and the cork go down as the air trapped inside the glass pushes the water down. A diving bell works in the same way.

Alexander the Great is said to have used a similar type of diving bell as early as 300 B.C. He had windows built into a tub so that he could see under the water.

Sometime later, large metal boxes were built to be used as workrooms under the water. These boxes had no bottoms, so the men had to stand in the water. Such diving bells were important to early builders of bridges, docks and harbors. Without them, underwater work would not have been possible.

In 1690, Sir Edmund Halley found that barrels of air could be taken down to a diving bell for the men to breathe. Now the men could stay underwater longer.

Later, a hose was fastened to the top of the diving bell so that air could be pumped to the men.

Today, workmen use air lock steel diving bells to work underwater. They climb down to the diving bell on a ladder inside a steel shaft. At the bottom, they open an airtight door and step into the air lock. A valve is opened to make the air pressure in the air lock the same as it was in the shaft. When the air pressure is the same, the men open another door and climb down into the working section of the diving bell. The air pressure in each part must be equalized before they can go to the next part.

Deep Sea Diving

Men need to move around while working in the ocean. Because a diving bell forced them to stay in one place, they soon began to make diving suits.

The first diving suits were made of leather. Today a suit is usually made of two layers of canvas with a layer of rubber between. It has tight rubber wrists and collar to keep it watertight. A diver wears a belt around his waist with lead weights on it. His strong boots have lead soles. They weigh over thirty pounds. The weights on his belt and his heavy boots help him stay upright as he walks along the ocean floor.

Before going underwater, the diver puts on a breastplate of copper. Then a copper helmet is fastened to the breastplate. It has thick plate-glass windows.

15

Inside the helmet is a telephone so that the men in the ship and the diver can talk to one another. There are also valves in the helmet to control the air coming through the air hose.

A deep-sea diver always works with a boat on the surface. A compressor on the boat compresses air and pumps it down to him through one of the two hoses attached to his helmet. The

other hose is his lifeline. When there is no telephone in the helmet, the diver pulls on the lifeline to signal the ship. If there is a telephone, the wires are inside the lifeline. The lifeline can also be used to pull him to the surface.

The deep-sea diver often carries tools and an electric light. He must be able to weld, cut metals, pour cement and do other underwater construction work. Sometimes deep-sea divers help raise sunken ships. Sometimes they recover lost treasures.

When a deep-sea diver is lowered from a boat, he goes straight down. His air hose and lifeline prevent him from walking very far from the place where he first touched bottom. He must be careful not to break or tangle his lines while working, for without them, he could not breathe or be pulled to safety in case of an emergency. His heavy suit and shoes, however, make it hard for him to move easily.

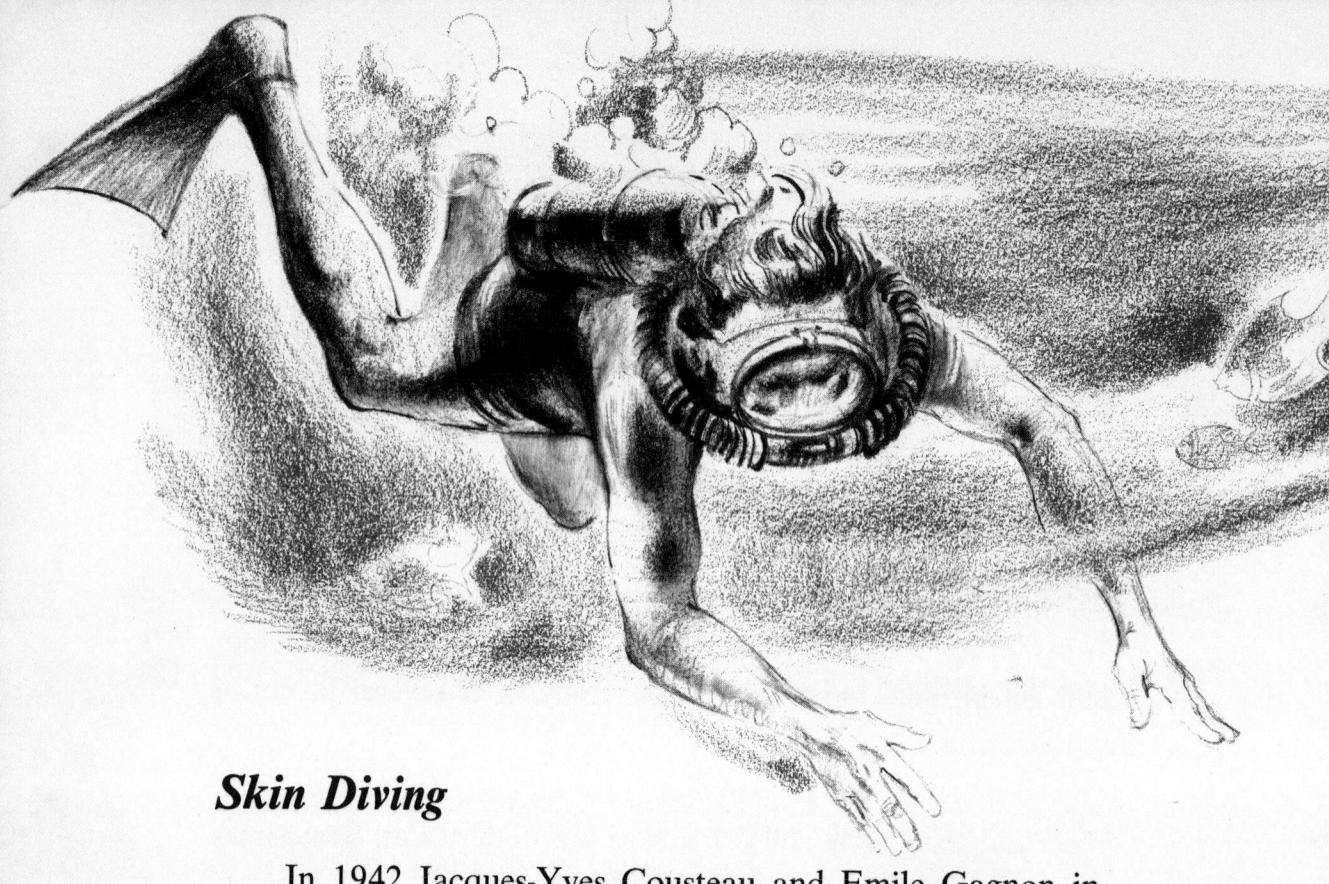

Skin Diving

In 1942 Jacques-Yves Cousteau and Emile Gagnon invented a new way to dive. They called it *skin diving* or *scuba diving*.

No longer did divers need to be tied to a ship by air hoses and lifelines or wear heavy diving suits. Most scuba divers wear only a bathing suit. On their backs they carry a tank of compressed air to breathe. They can swim wherever they want to. Scuba divers, however, cannot go as far underwater as deep-sea divers.

Above the tanks of compressed air on the diver's back is an air valve that controls the flow of air. Two hoses carry the air to a mouthpiece through which the diver gets air. Used air escapes in bubbles. Divers wear a face mask to keep water out of their eyes and nose and to make it easier to see.

When the water is cold, the scuba diver wears a rubber *wet suit*. A little water gets inside of a wet suit, forming a layer to help keep him warm. In very cold water, divers wear a *dry suit*. It fits tightly around the neck, wrists and ankles so that no water can get inside. Under the dry suit they wear several layers of woolen underwear.

Entire families go skin diving for the fun of exploring coral reefs and seeing colorful fish and plants underwater. Sometimes they catch lobsters and shellfish with their hands, or they shoot fish with a speargun.

Scuba divers do underwater construction work and help raise sunken ships. Sometimes they search for deposits of oil or other minerals in the ocean. They also take pictures of undersea life.

Naval skin divers are called *frogmen*. Almost all countries have used them to lay mines, blow up bridges and help rescue submarines. During World War II, Italian frogmen were able to sink an English battleship.

The Submarine

The first successful submarine was built in England in 1620 by Cornelis Drebbel. For the next four years, he made many trips beneath the waters of the Thames River at depths of twelve to fifteen feet.

King James I is said to have taken a ride in Drebbel's submarine, which consisted of a small wooden frame covered with waterproofed leather. Oars stuck out of its side so that it could be rowed from inside. Leather flaps kept the water from coming in at the oar holes.

The American Colonies were the first to use a submarine to attack a ship in wartime. During the Revolutionary War, David Bushnell built a one-man submarine. It was a wooden, pear-shaped boat and was run by a hand-cranked propeller. It was called *The Turtle*.

In 1776, *The Turtle* was used in New York Harbor to try to sink a British man-of-war. The attempt was not successful but it forced the British to move their ships out of the harbor.

The first submarines were very small. Today submarines can carry over 100 men and can go around the world without surfacing. The newest, run by nuclear energy, do not even have to stop for fuel.

Most submarines have been built for warfare or for the protection of a country. Some of the new United States' submarines carry Polaris guided missiles for use against ships or coastal cities. Future submarines might someday carry freight.

Submarines do not lend themselves to underwater exploration. They are built without windows in order to make them strong. They are guided by *sonar*, a navigational aid that bounces sound waves off underwater objects. A periscope is used when the crew wants to look around. Submarines are too large to be used in exploring and can only go down to a depth of about 500 feet.

Bathysphere

Scientists have always wanted to explore the deeper parts of the ocean, but were prevented from doing so because of the effects of water pressure. Water is heavy and will crush even a submarine if it dives too deeply.

Two scientists, William Beebe and Otis Barton, dreamed of exploring the ocean floor, and drew up plans for a round steel ball that would withstand water pressure at great depths. The ball, which they called a *bathysphere,* was fastened to a long steel cable so that it could be lowered into the ocean from a ship.

On August 15, 1934, the two men were lowered into the water near Bermuda in their bathysphere to a depth of 3,000 feet. It was the deepest underwater dive on record and would not be bettered for fifteen years. As they descended, Beebe and Barton reported that the color of the ocean changed from a brilliant blue to a dark blue-black and that they saw many luminous sea creatures glowing in the dark water. They noticed light gleaming from what appeared to be tiny portholes along the bodies of some fish. Others looked as if they were covered with silver tinsel.

The bathysphere could not, of course, be made to move around by itself. It had to be pulled on its cable from the ship. There was always danger of the cable breaking or becoming tangled as it bumped along on the ocean floor.

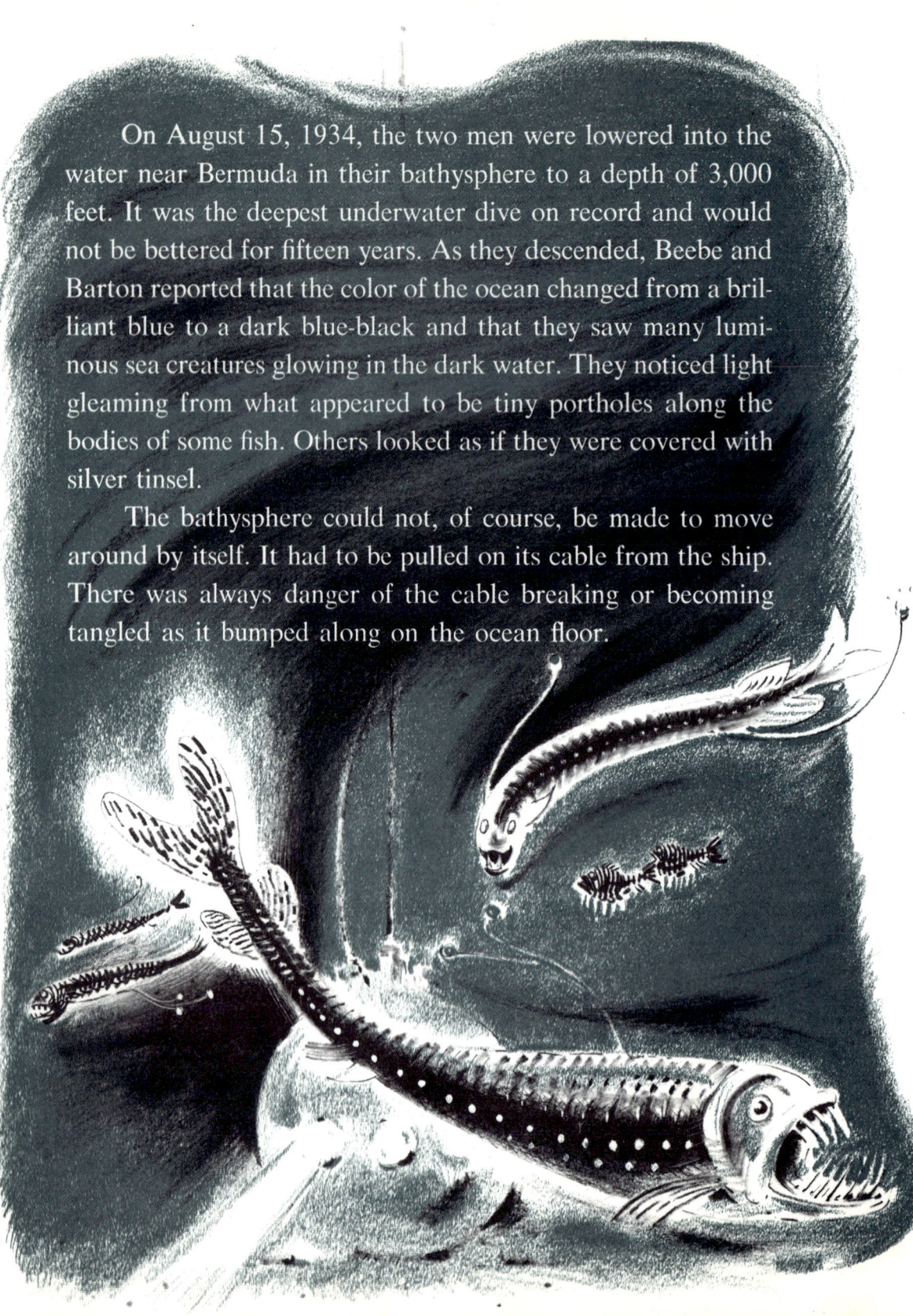

The Bathyscaphe

Although the bathysphere enabled men to explore a little of the ocean depths, it had many drawbacks. A scientist named Auguste Piccard drew up plans for a better kind of deep-water boat which he called a *bathyscaphe*. It was finished in 1948 and could dive and return to the surface under its own power.

Piccard's bathyscaphe contained many large tanks. Some were filled with gasoline, which, being lighter than water, gave them buoyancy. Others could be filled with sea water to make them sink. When the men in the bathyscaphe wanted to return to the surface, some of this sea water was pumped out again. The men rode in a plexiglass sphere fastened under the craft.

Auguste Piccard built several bathyscaphes before he was able to make a successful deep dive in 1954. The United States Navy became interested in one of his bathyscaphes, *The Trieste,* which they bought and took to the Pacific Ocean. On January 23, 1960, at the Marianas Trench, thought to be the deepest spot in the Pacific Ocean, Jacques Piccard and Lieutenant Donald Walsh dived to a depth of 35,800 feet — almost seven miles down into the ocean.

Submersibles

Today a new type of vehicle is exploring the ocean bottom. Bathyscaphes are able only to go up and down. The new vehicles, some built with large port-holes and others with windows, are called *submersibles* and can move around freely underwater. The United States government and individual manufacturers are building submersibles. In them, scientists are studying animal life and ocean currents and are scouting for fish, oil and minerals. Men can work long hours underwater using the moveable arms, powerful lights and television cameras with which most submersibles are equipped.

In 1970, a team of scientists, headed by Jacques Piccard, studied the Gulf Stream in a submersible named *Ben Franklin*. Piccard called this underwater vehicle a *mesoscaph* or middle-boat. The scientists drifted in the Gulf Stream for thirty days covering a distance of 1,500 miles. They were surprised to find that the Gulf Stream contained very little marine life.

In 1969, the United States Navy launched *NR-1*, the first nuclear-powered submersible. It can stay underwater a month because it does not depend upon batteries for its power. The Navy Department is still keeping secret most of the operational details of this five-man vehicle.

Submersibles can be used for work other than oceanographic research. They have been used to recover important objects lost at sea. In 1966, the submersibles, *Alvin* and *Aluminaut*, helped recover an unexploded hydrogen bomb lost in deep water off the coast of Spain. In 1969, *Deep Quest* recovered the flight and voice recorders from two airplanes that crashed in the Pacific

Ocean after taking off from Los Angeles. Scientists are now working on a deep diving submersible which will be able to go down to 20,000 feet to rescue men trapped in submarines.

The Naval Undersea Warfare Center operates several underwater robots. These cable-controlled vehicles are equipped with television cameras, lights, sonar and a large claw to use in picking up objects such as torpedoes, mines and bombs which are too dangerous to be handled by men in a submersible. One of these robots did the actual picking up of the hydrogen bomb lost near Spain after it had been dragged to shallow water by *Alvin* and *Aluminaut*.

Too Many People

In the last 25 years, men have learned more about the oceans than in all of the years before. What will they do with this knowledge?

Today there is reason to fear that our world is becoming over-populated. We are rapidly using up our supplies of coal, iron, oil and other important minerals. In some parts of the world, people are hungry because there is not enough food. By the year 2,000, experts say that there may not be room enough on earth for all the people.

Where will these people live? How will they get food and shelter? Will some of them go to the moon or to another planet to live?

Some scientists believe that the oceans can solve some of these problems. There are minerals in and under the oceans. Iron, gold and diamonds are on the ocean bottom. We are already making use of some of these. In the future, we may be able to use even more.

We usually think of men fishing for food with lines and nets, but in Japan, people raise fish in ocean pens. They do not have to go out in boats seeking fish. The Japanese and other peoples of Asia also harvest seaweed for food. Rich in nutrients, it is a valuable addition to their diet.

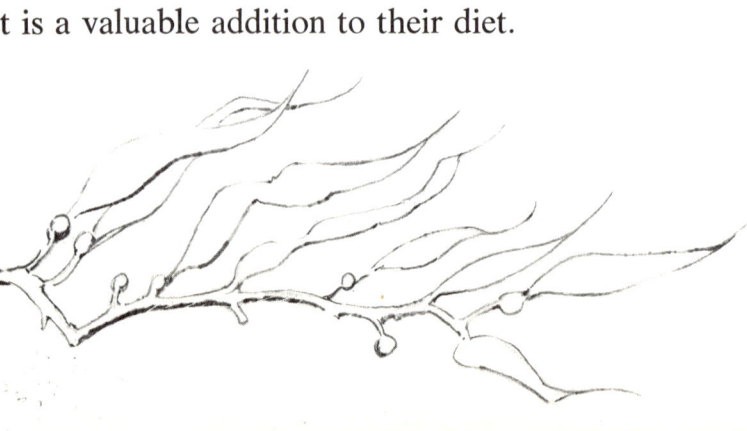

TRUMBULL COUNTY
LIBRARY SERVICE
WARREN, OHIO

Conshelf

Some scientists believe that men can live in the oceans, and that some day there can be cities on the bottom of the sea. The famous underwater explorer, Captain Jacques-Yves Cousteau is one of the men who is trying to find ways for people to live in the ocean. He has made experiments in living on the *continental shelf*, that ledge of ocean floor beneath the shallower water that surrounds earth's continents. Most of the fish and plants in the ocean grow on the continental shelves where the sun's rays reach to the bottom. Captain Cousteau called his project *Conshelf*.

The first part of the Conshelf project was carried out in 1962, when two men lived for seven days in a tiny house at a depth of thirty-three feet.

In the summer of 1963, Captain Cousteau began a new project. He and his men built a house which they called *Starfish*. They wanted to put it on the bottom of the Red Sea.

First, divers went down to level and smooth the ocean floor. Next they sank *Starfish* forty feet to the bottom of the sea and tied it in place. They used heavy weights to keep the house from floating away. It stood on long legs seven feet above the floor of the Red Sea.

Inside *Starfish* were a television set, a telephone, a shower, beds, and a place to eat and cook. The men who lived there could do almost anything in their house that you can do in yours.

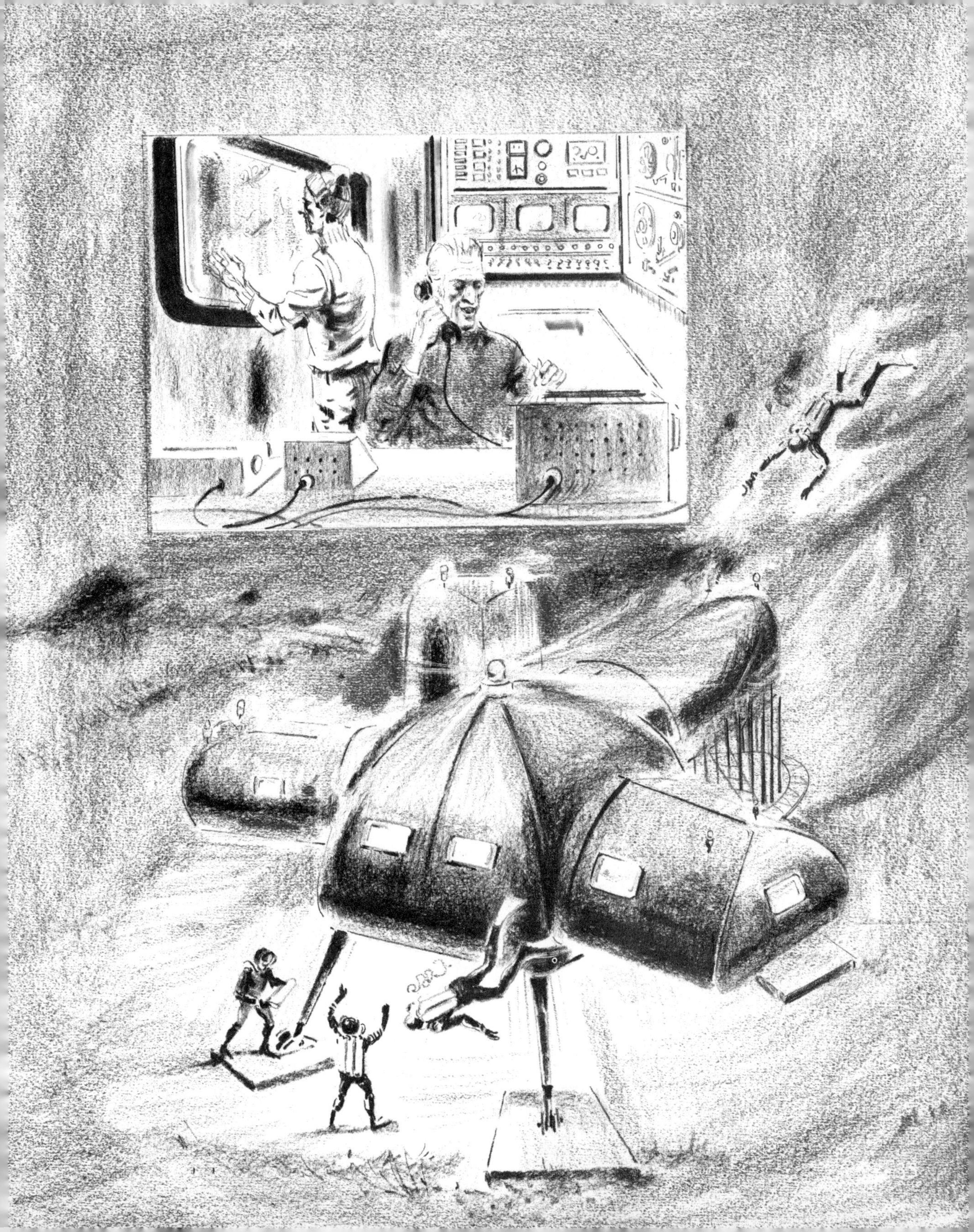

They also had an underwater garage for their submersible, which Captain Cousteau called a diving saucer because of its shape. They used the diving saucer for exploring the bottom of the Red Sea.

In 1965, Captain Cousteau and five other men lived for three weeks in a house anchored at a depth of 328 feet. In all of these projects, the men used scuba diving equipment to work underwater and then returned to their underwater house.

Captain Cousteau believes that these projects prove that humans can live and work on the ocean floor.

Man-in-the-Sea

United States scientists are working on a similar project called *Man-in-the-Sea*. The *Sea-Labs* are part of this project.

In 1964, four men lived 193 feet underwater for eleven days in *Sea-Lab I*. The "habitat," as they called the metal cylinder they lived in, was anchored off Bermuda. Every day the men put on diving outfits and swam out into the ocean. There they collected marine samples, made studies of currents and water temperatures and did tasks that tested man's ability to work underwater at different depths.

A year later, three teams of ten men each lived 205 feet down in the water in *Sea-Lab II*. Each team lived there for fifteen days. The habitat was now anchored off the coast of California.

The teams of *Sea-Lab* again worked in the ocean. A trained porpoise named Tuffy came to the divers whenever he heard a buzzer. Tuffy brought them tools and supplies. He also brought their mail each day. In one experiment, the porpoise swam to the surface and back down to the habitat seven times in twenty minutes. Tuffy was trained to find lost divers and could have brought a man to the surface in an emergency.

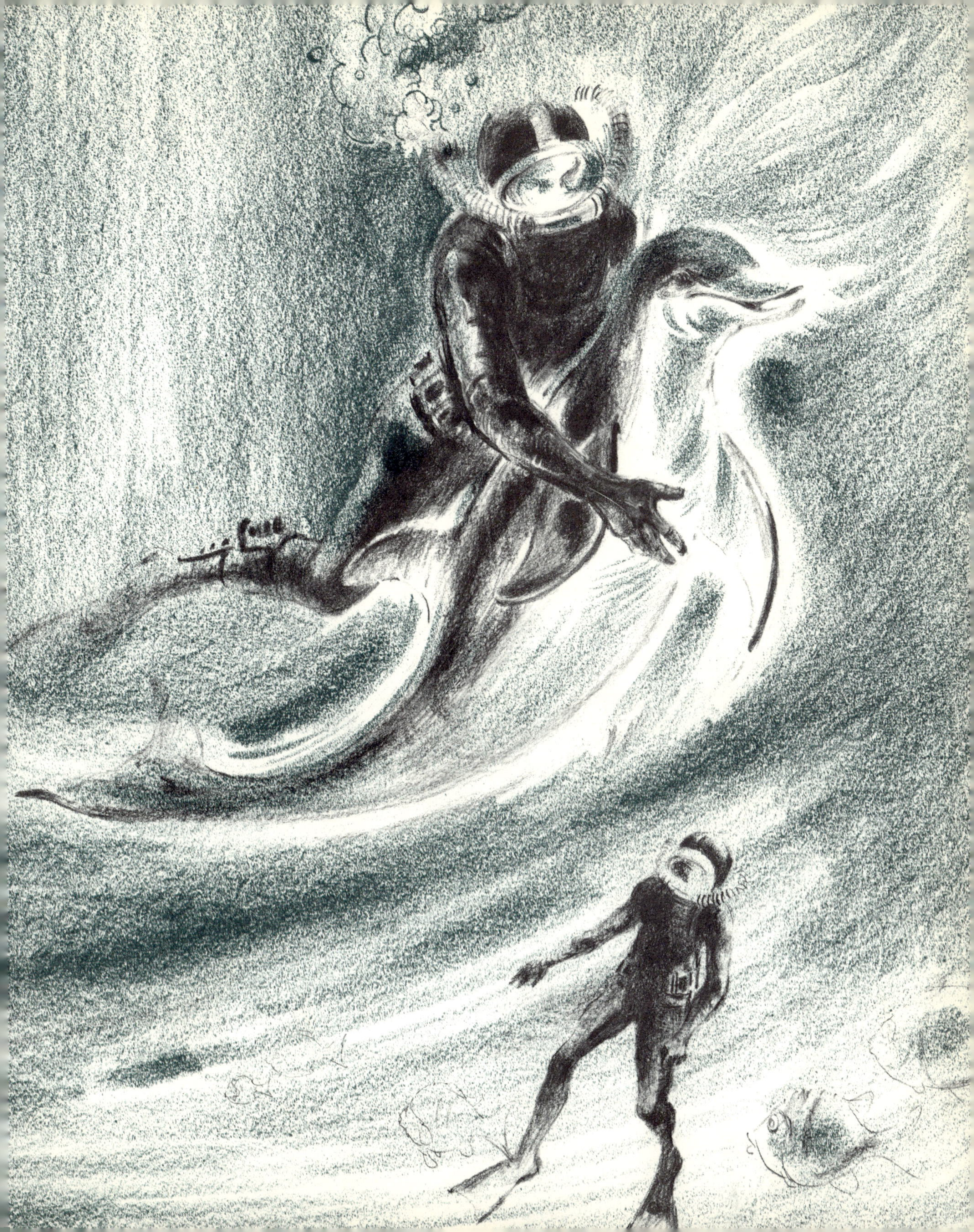

Sea-Lab III was begun off the coast of California early in 1969. In addition to Tuffy, it had three other trained animals — two porpoises and a sea-lion — which had been taught to help the divers in their work. Five teams of eight men each planned to live for twelve days each at a depth of 600 feet. Unfortunately, the project had to be abandoned because one of the divers died on his descent to the Sea-Lab unit. It was later determined that his death had been due to faulty diving equipment.

At about the same time, another Man-in-the-Sea project began in the Atlantic Ocean called *Tektite I*. Here, in an underwater experiment off the Virgin Islands, four men lived for sixty days at a depth of 42 feet.

Tektite II involved 62 scientists who took turns during the summer and fall of 1970 living at a depth of fifty feet beneath the warm Caribbean waters. One team was composed of five women.

Although these projects have shown that men can live and work in the ocean, there are still problems to be solved.

A team of British scientists have drawn up plans for an underwater city of 30,000 people to be enclosed in a glass dome. It would contain stores, apartment houses, a firehouse, a hospital and places for people to swim out to raise food in ocean gardens and pens. Such cities could be built in parts of the ocean where the water is not too deep nor the tides too high. They say that one could be constructed now, but they admit that it will probably not come about for another fifty years.

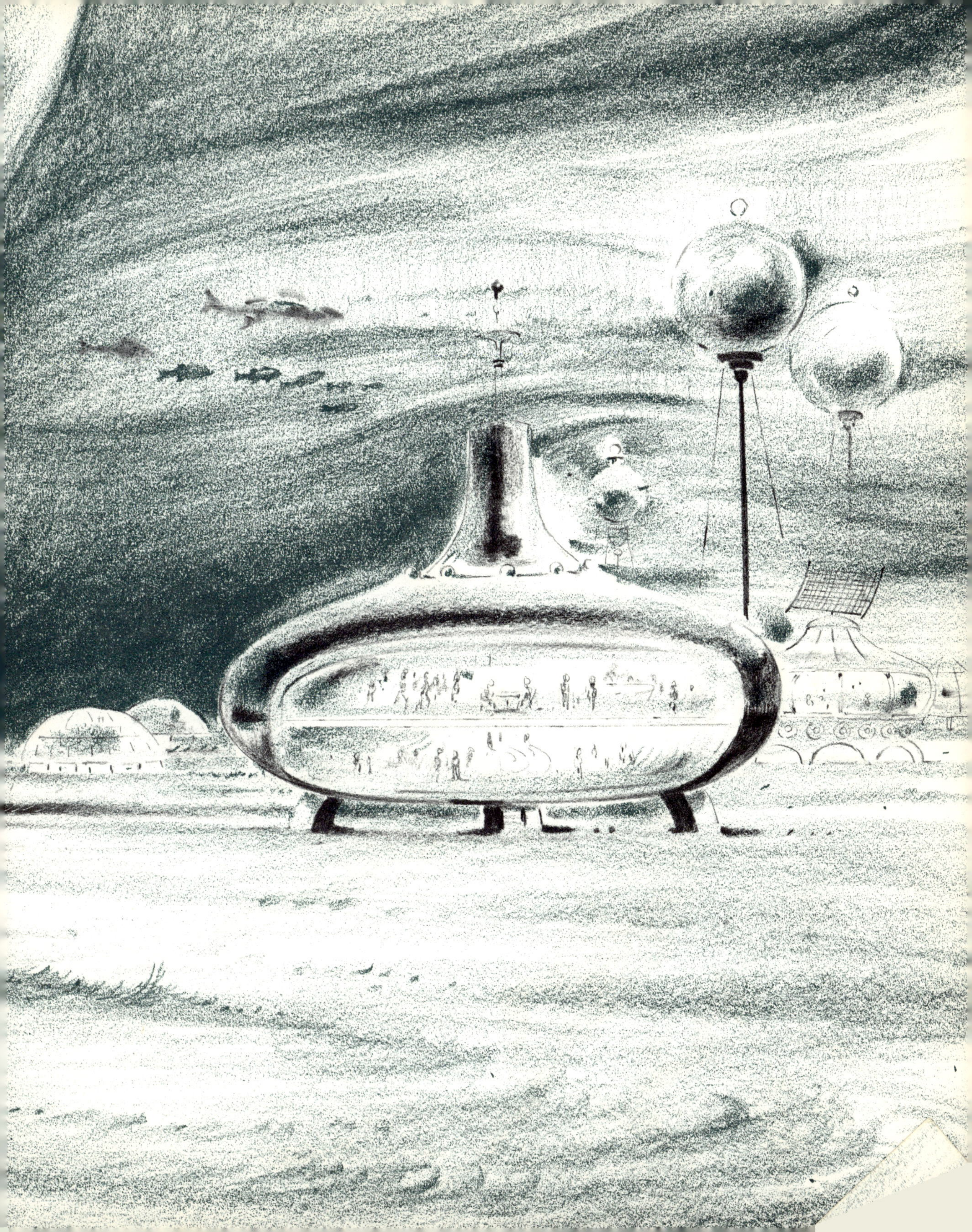

Some scientists, on the other hand, believe that underwater cities need not be encased in a glass dome. They say people could use diving outfits and submersibles to go from their houses to other places.

Some day you may live under the sea in a city in a house much like *Starfish*. You may keep fish in a pen to eat or perhaps as pets. Your garden may be of seaweed. Maybe your car will look like the diving saucer. Or perhaps you will swim to school every morning in a diving outfit.

INDEX

Air pressure, 11, 14
Alexander the Great, 12
Aluminaut, 30-31
Alvin, 30-31

Barton, Otis, 25-26
Bathyscaphe, 27-28
Bathysphere, 25-26
Beebe, William, 25-26
Ben Franklin, 28
Bushnell, David, 23

Conshelf, 34, 36-37
Continental shelf, 34
Cousteau, Jacques-Yves, 18, 34, 36-37

Deep Quest, 30
Deep sea diving, 15-17
Deep sea diving suits, 15-17
Diving bells, 11-14
Diving saucer, 36, 44
Drebbel, Cornelis, 23
Dry suit, 19

Frogmen, 20

Gagnon, Emile, 18
Gulf Stream, 28

Halley, Sir Edmund, 13

James I (of England), 23

Man-in-the-Sea, 38, 40-41
Marianas Trench, 27
Mesoscaph, 28

NR-1, 30
Naval Undersea Warfare Center, 31

Pearl diving, 10
Piccard, Auguste, 27
Piccard, Jacques, 27-28
Polaris guided missiles, 24
Population, 32

Red Sea, 34, 36
Revolutionary War, 23

Scuba diving, 18-20
Sea-Lab I, 38
Sea-Lab II, 38
Sea-Lab III, 40
Skin diving. 18-20
Sonar, 24
Starfish house, 34, 44
Submarines, 23-24
Submersibles, 28, 30-31

Tektite I, 40-41
Tektite II, 41
Trieste, 27
Tuffy, 38, 40
Turtle, 23

Underwater city, 42, 44
Underwater robots, 31

Walsh, Lieutenant Donald, 27
Water cycle, 10
Wet suit, 19

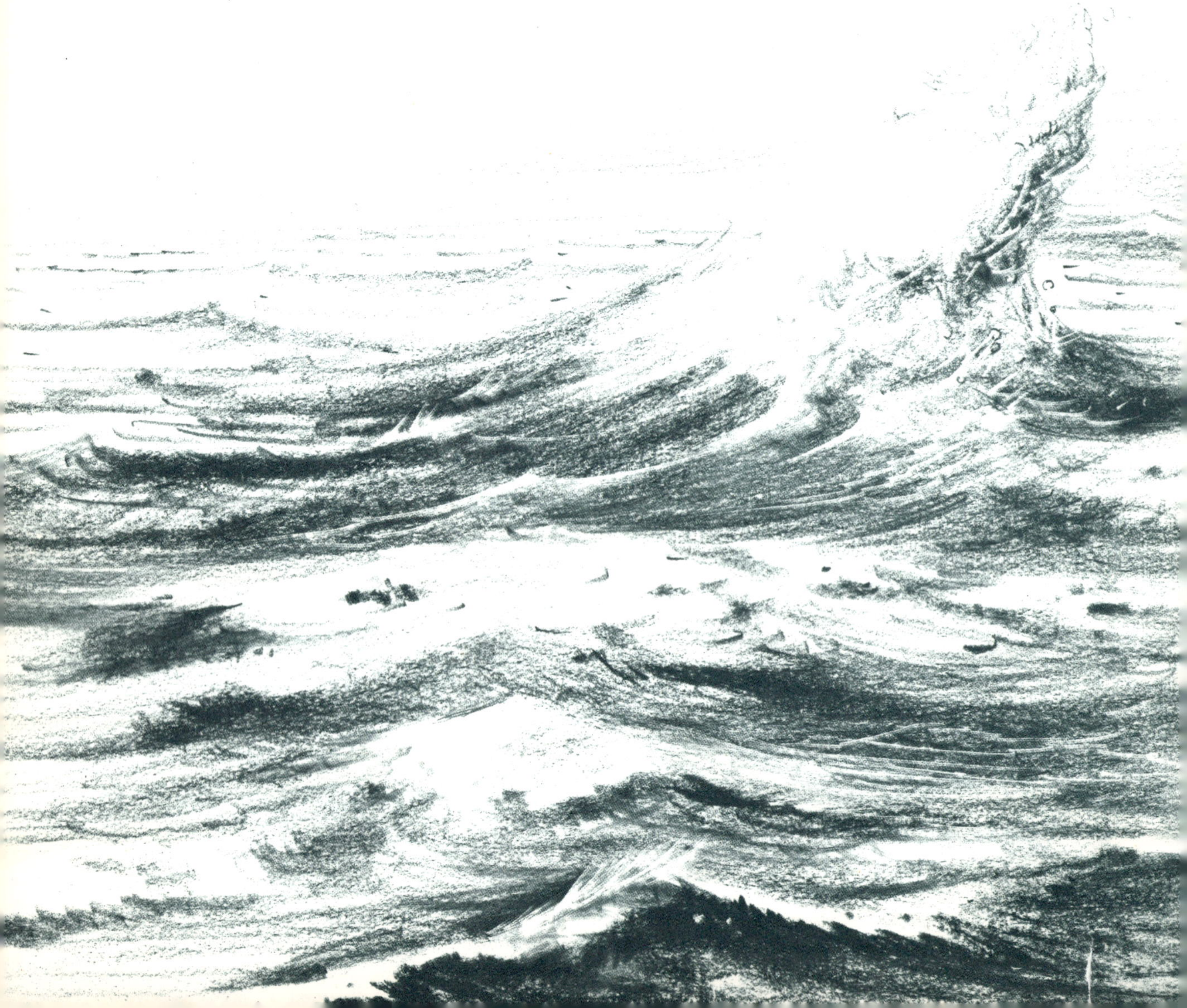

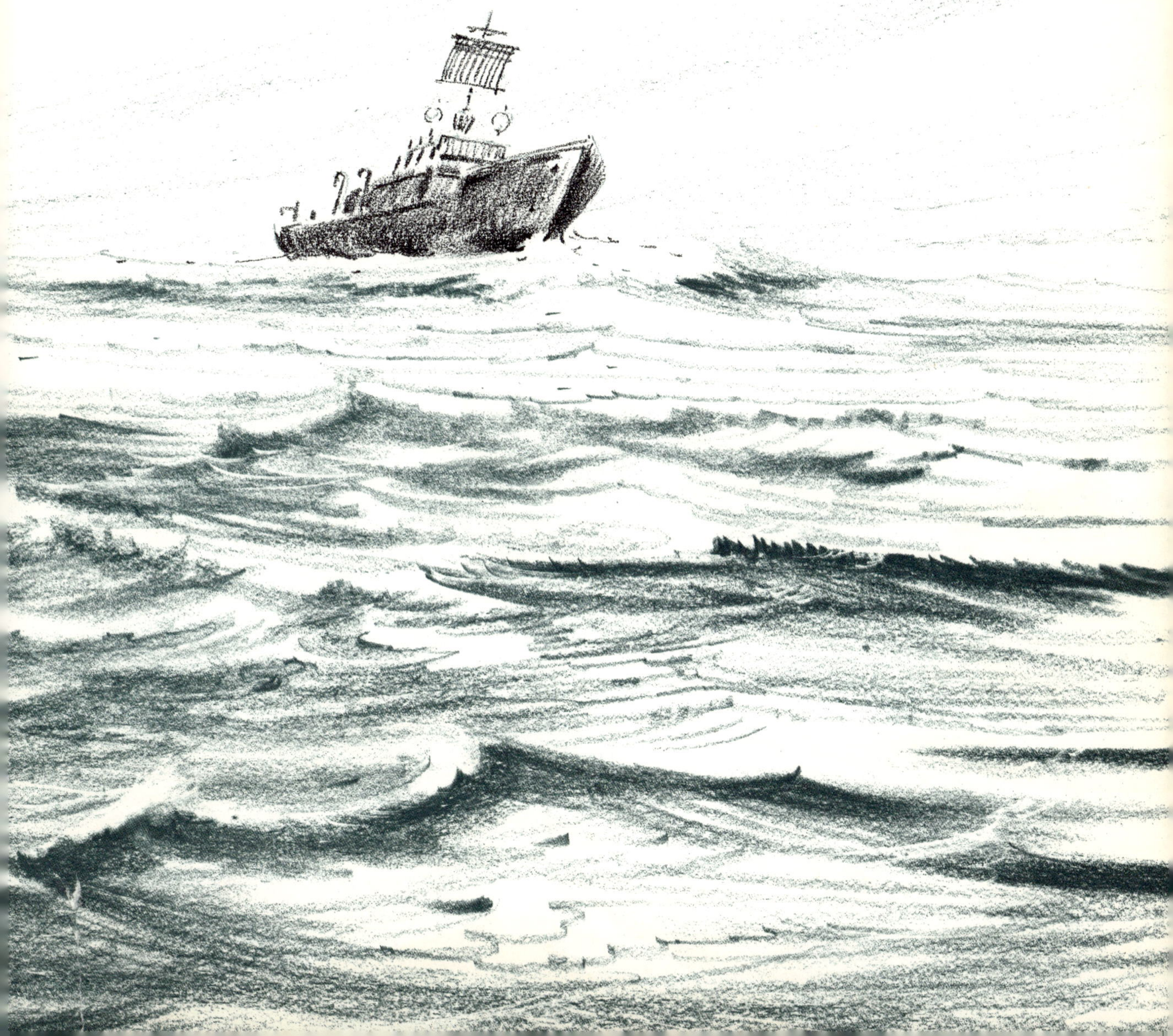

About the Author

A graduate of Humboldt State College in California, Anabel Dean has also done graduate work at the University of California and at Chico State College. During summer vacations she has travelled extensively in Mexico, Central America, Europe, Africa, and Asia, as well as in the United States. Currently she is a teacher in the primary grades in Redding, California, where she and her husband and their three children make their home.

About the Artist

Vincent Colabella is known as a versatile illustrator of books and educational filmstrips. Four of his filmstrips were awarded the 1968 Grand Trophy at the International Film and Television Festival. He is a graduate of Pratt Institute School of Fine and Applied Arts in Brooklyn. He resides with his family in Westchester County, New York.